THE RENTED VIOLIN

THE RENTED VIOLIN

Karen Whalley

AUSABLE PRESS
2003

Cover art: Ben Stechschulte (Polaroid).
Design and composition by Ausable Press.
The type is Adobe's Jenson with Trajan titling.
Cover design by Rebecca Soderholm.

Published by
AUSABLE PRESS
1026 HURRICANE ROAD, KEENE NY 12942-9712
www.ausablepress.com

Distributed by
SMALL PRESS DISTRIBUTION
800-869-7553
www.spdbooks.org

The acknowledgments appear on page 87 and constitute
a continuation of the copyrights page.

Library of Congress Cataloging-in-Publication Data
Whalley, Karen
The rented violin : poems / Karen Whalley. –1st ed.
p. cm.
ISBN 1-931337-13-6 (hardcover : alk. paper)
ISBN 1-931337-14-4 (pbk. : alk. paper)
I. Title.
PS3623.H36R46 2003
811'.6–dc22

2003015473

for Christopher
and for Tony Hoagland

THE RENTED VIOLIN

I.

YELLOW FROM A DISTANCE

We have almost reached the pond;
You have left your glasses at home on the table
And squint across the field
To the unfolding skunk cabbage.
Farsighted or near, I can't remember which
But you say it is only yellow you see,
Which from a distance could be daffodils.
But they are different shapes, the bell and the candle,
And I describe to you how they float
On the marsh, like a harbor of lanterns,
Because I want you to see them as I do,
A thousand tiny sails, each distinct,
Each one among the others, each drifting.

To you, the world's a blur, and I recall another walk
When the cherry trees had lifted their pink awnings
And you couldn't see the trees themselves,
Only the row of cloudy blossoms passing overhead—
Happy for that much. I think sometimes
You leave them off,
Not because you love my voice
As we pass each yard with its scrubby patch of flowers,
Or how I tell the shades of blue,
But because the earth is beautiful,
And beauty is a form of suffering.

FALLING

An overweight woman
With a big hairdo
Is blow-drying my dog
And telling me about a retreat
She's just flown back from
Called *Weekend of Trust*
Or *Two Days of Falling
Into Arms of Strangers.*
Her shop is a mess,
And I'm trying to imagine
Being three times my size
And how you'd have to bathe
And bathe when you showered,
Like a job you can't quit.
Try bending through three people
Just to sweep or to weed.

Imagine, she tells me,
*Being in a room as big as a gym
With sixty people you've never met.*
I remember covering the soft cup
In my son's scalp for months
Until the cranium's gate slid shut.
And, sometimes, I fold my arms

Beneath my breasts when I think
I might weep. *Imagine,* she tells me,
Five plastic chairs stacked
And having to climb them.
The wobbly kind, she adds,
So I know this is a true story
About disaster and its matching sock,
Salvation. I imagine a small tree
With one thin branch,
And there's me in it. Wind,
There'd have to be armloads of wind.

The group leader tells her,
Now just fall back. We'll catch you.
The woman grasps the only rope
Of her life and can't fall back,
Though everyone is chanting
And a lot of arms are urging her down
As if a fireman's unfolding a ladder
To the roof of a tall building.
When she does fall,
They rock her in a hammock
Like she's never been rocked,
Not in infancy, not in a grown man's cradle,

Not that tenderness.
I can't help myself but lie back
Into all the arms I've lain in
So when it was my turn to hold, I could:
That widowed friend, that college boy
I rocked in a narrow dormitory cot,
That baby that made a bed of me.

HOLLYHOCKS

The moment a man questions the meaning of his life, he is sick.
                —Sigmund Freud

I don't remember when I stopped
Questioning. Maybe it was when
My neighbor Marge lost her daughter
To cancer, buried without her hair.
Marge didn't mention it
When she carried a bowl
Of cherry tomatoes over
And stood in the cidery shade
Of a small-leafed tree, not talking
Across the fence. *This heat's blinding,*
She said, and held a long salute
Above her eyes, twisting her sad
Gray braid into a knot at the nape.
Why didn't she say something?

I look a little foolish as I look
Back now, standing waist-deep in yarrow,
Happy as a hat, checking for leaf miners,
As if we both had time enough
To speculate the way we did
On what color you'd call the hollyhocks.
As if pink weren't enough of a word.
Maybe what she needed

When the call came from Idaho
Was to pick a bowl of cold tomatoes.
Maybe she needed to be
Any old woman in the world but her
Stooping to tall hollyhocks
And searching her mind
For just the right shade of pink.

LOVE MUST BE ACTUAL

It has its own day on the calendar
Like Jesus' birth, or Lincoln's.
Maybe hope is a star
They were both born under;
Maybe grace is a constellation.
Today, love is actual flowers,
White daisies and red carnations,
Stems a wrist in a plastic sleeve
Where love's colors gather
Like a promise at a high-school dance,
Girls bunched along a wall for picking,
The gym an elixir of shy perfumes.
I fluff them in a vase.
I water them in awe.

We have our habits. You like to tear
Bread, I like to slice it.
You tear it and hold a piece
To my mouth. I say, *It's awkward*
To eat from someone else's hand.
But I do, and I do.
The way deer let trees
Hold our scabbed winter apples.
Half at a time, that's how
They take one. And the tree not holding.
And the little stumble of lips.

Later, I'll stay here reading
As you climb the stairs to bed,
Another habit we've lost to,
Like the dog orbiting her rug
Molding a bowl for her body to fill.
How willingly we enter whatever will hold us:
This tea's turned a cup shape,
This cup takes my hand looping the handle,
My lips searching the rim.
You, I know it, are swimming into sleep.
I put on a slow song
To make another country
And, Lord, I'm lost
We're in so deep.

TWO TRUE STORIES

It is better to save yourself
Than to save another person.
I write this at forty
After a man I loved
Spiraled toward his own destruction
The way, just now, a solitary leaf
Feathered its way down to impeccable grass.

I think there must be a voice
In even a leaf—
Nothing grand, nothing outlandish—
Just a flutter of breath
From holding on with its one thin arm
To the tree; who of us knows for how long?

There is something beautiful
About the way a drunk sleeps.
Such calm. Such stillness.
He had pressed his hands together
Like a pillow, and I think this is the way
The dead sleep, if we could see them.
No desire. No concupiscence.

When I was eleven,
My friend's father slept in his vomit
In the front seat of their green Valiant,
Though I now remember
His black hair was thoughtfully combed.
What did I know about alcohol, then?
My friend looked in the window
Of the car at her sleeping father
And said, *That bastard.*

I remember, too, when the man I tried to save
Made a sandwich for himself in my kitchen,
Carefully cutting it in half
As if propriety dictated this precision.
The deliberate motion of his trembling hand.

AFTER FOUR YEARS

Once, I saw him crossing
The street at dusk, after his shop
Was locked, the *Closed* sign turned
Against the window, the day's
Receipts tucked into the bank bag,
And the last customer had shuffled
Into the anonymous faces on the sidewalk.

I didn't recognize him—I was that detached—
Didn't say *Hello*, but afterward
That feeling of familiarity made me stop
And turn around, made me think
Husband to the old, sad shape of him
Imprinted still in memory.
I watched him cross, lonely boat, through
A river of traffic.

When do we stop caring
About the way the story ends?
When he left, he left for good.
Maybe I could give him now
What I wasn't able to give him then.

In the ledger of my omissions,
He is the biggest entry:

We were never as good as we think we were,
And we were always better.

Somewhere, in a gray dusk,
I am always the woman washing dishes;
He is always the man kneeling
At the border of the garden,
Laying the thick, curled rope of edging
At the lip, packing the dirt tight
On the bare side of the grass.
I see us over and over.
It is how we loved each other.

AT THE BACK

My friend, as we talk, is swinging
Her two-year-old daughter
In a tree swing. It is early December,
And what's left of the light
Is failing fast, so we are less
Visible to each other, more
Palpable, our voices almost inaudible now.
In the foreign country of childhood
Someone must have said,
At this hour, in this particular kind of light,
Quiet, or you'll wake your father.
Hush, or you'll wake the baby.

Each strict branch arches the air
And between the few leaves left
The blue sky blackens, like a bruise.
It's still beautiful, the sparks starting
In the one big ember, the fractured half-dark,
Just as the last night I spent in Rome
Seemed like *it* was leaving *me*,
And I couldn't sleep
Because it was a kind of relinquishment.

It would be easy to walk
Away from all this: the imperfect weather

And the imperfect night, the way a man walks
Out of the house because he just doesn't love her
        anymore,
Or the way a woman turns silent in order
To leave but not leave,
But this is a moment when everything I love
Hurts me to not be holding:
Friends scattered, like wreckage, across the country,
The lives I've lived and lost.

Each time Lael sails back to her mother's hands
She says, *Hi, Momma,*
Then flies skyward, only to return
And say it again,
As if she is proving a theory of physics,
researching a degree of certainty.
Imagine having someone's hands
Be everything you need on earth.

FRENCH ROSE

It is the day after Thanksgiving,
The year terrorists
Toppled two buildings in the name of religion
And gave Americans the gift
Of humility and took from them a certain innocence.
It is the year
In which I fell out of love—
Or he fell out of love with me,
Which is really the long angel's fall
From grace, from the heaven
A good feeling makes between two people,
And I learned redemption
Is passing up the opportunity
To stay in pain.

I am watching the apple tree
Drop precisely one apple per day,
As if it has mastered the beautiful art
Of giving up, and in that nudity
It is free of red ornaments,
Like the vulnerable face
Of a woman without lipstick
Who has made her peace
With the pretenses of the world.

I am poor and single.
I am poor and married
To the idea of happiness, the same way *sky*
Is the only word for *blue*.
Because it's my birthday,
I bathed this morning
In the French rose soap
My sister bought for me
At a ritzy store in an upscale mall,
Proving there is a world
Where people care about the way things smell
And the delicate carved *M*
In the top of the bar
Like a secret initial to some exclusive club
So that a woman like myself
Might rise one morning
From the sweet and steamy bath
Into cold November air,
Slick and pink from the hot water
Ready to begin again with a faith
Odd as a terrorist's, thinking, *This is how you live, this*
Is what you do.

STILL LIFE IN FROST

If I could paint
I'd be in my back yard right now
Unfolding an easel into unfolding dawn,
Planting a chair dead center,
Like the hub of a wheel lacquered in frost,
A wool beret, a blue one,
Cocked at an angle
So I would summon artistic thoughts,
Perhaps a scarf wound against the dampness.
Perhaps I'd lift a cigarette
Contemplatively to my lips
As if I were tasting a glass
Of rare and expensive European Chardonnay,
Tasting it and tasting it to better hear
The dry, sweet language of the tongue.

Maybe I'd just study the view
Before dipping my brush into the palette
Of choices, noticing first how the side of a wall
Goes dark to light then dark again
With the swift, accidental passage of a cloud,
Not recording it on canvas, just practicing
Seeing for the sake of itself,
Or how the rose hips look suddenly

Sexual and blood-gorged
On the stripped husks
Of the Chinese hexagrams of the hedge.

Maybe I'd invent a way
Of turning the song of an ordinary bird
Into a color and a shape:
Just above the roof,
Like a book turned face down,
Three yellow splashes, like bright nails
Holding the page of this morning to the world.

LAZARUS

By March, the leaves are budding
On the dogwood; the bulb species
Is resurrecting in tight green scrolls.

Gardens aren't natural: what I mean is,
Someone had to put them there. Someone
Carried a basket through a nursery

And chose from among the many plants,
This violet, say, for its lacy flowers,
This tulip for its flagrant, lipstick red.

So many others left on the shelf,
Like books you'll never get to read,
Or like the puppy at the pound

Whose large paws foretold
A future of uncontainable joy
For which your house felt too small.

In this way, only, we resemble God,
Deciding what goes and what stays
As the water rises around us,

Which is our life going under.
For instance, this morning
I dug last year's perennial geranium

From the ground to put in a meadow rue.
That quickly, desire had changed
Something already good into something

Not much better, which is enough,
Almost, to make me satisfied
With what I already have,

Which is spring and this feeling
Like sinking, that nothing ever ends
And that nothing ever lasts.

WILD GINGER

He'd gone to the men's room
And I was watching the cook
At the open grill
Threading strips of lamb onto skewers,
Little whiffs of smoke rising
As impaled flesh hit flame,
And the crackle of fat
Was like static
In the clusters of conversation.

I sat there, wondering what I was doing
In that room,
Waiting for a man
The way I used to wait for my father
As he took some drunk to lunch
Because *Jesus would have shown that kind of compassion.*

I didn't want to be sitting there,
And I didn't want to get up and leave
Or to think what I was thinking then:
That women are supposed to wait for men,
And men are supposed to disappear
To see if a woman
Is appropriately patient
As a man is being approximately himself.

And when he finally did emerge
From the door with *Men's Room*
Painted in gold script,
He was strutting—
That kind of cocky walk
A man does that says,
This is the world of men
And no woman can enter here.
The kind of strut
That says, *A woman is waiting for me,*
And the woman doesn't matter,
Because he's doing it for other men.

RUNAWAY

On a ferry, a handsome tall man
wearing a ring, maybe on his way home
To his wife, self-assured enough he could have chosen
Anyone, looked and looked at me,
And what did he see there? I wanted
To see what he saw, but I saw only him,
Passing so closely we could have walked
Into each other's arms, could have made
A history of passions, like the ancient Greeks.

I know a woman who believes that,
Of the billions of people on this planet,
There is only one for each of us,
Like a twin searching for its other,
Like a dog looking for its bowl,
Like a bed holding the imprint of a body
Long after the body is gone. We pray
And we prey.

And, once, a male friend put his hand
On my thigh as he was driving—not groping,
But thoughtlessly letting his hand
Fall where it wanted. I still love that moment:
The two of us affectionate, the *almost*

Of it, the endless possibility. And I'm not certain,
Tonight, it would have been immoral
For us to stop at a roadside motel
With tasteless paintings on the walls
And the tiny bar of pink soap and wrapped glasses
At the sink and just lie down together. Or, simply stop
The car and undress in our seats
Parked at an overlook where the lights
Of some strange city glowed below, before driving on.

Remember when Jimmy Carter said
He had lusted in his heart? A heart
With a little lust in it never hurt anyone—
Even lust is the stirring of an old tenderness.

Recently, a man in what we call *a committed*
Relationship asked if I'd sleep with him.
I couldn't imagine those hands, that mouth
On me. Immediately, he was sorry,
With the face and posture of a child's at a dinner party
Who has spilled the milk, wanting to dissolve
Into the flowers of the wallpaper behind him. I almost
        wish I had.

I almost wish I had spared him that,
And let him, right there, in the afterglow
Of a lovely dinner at a fine restaurant, maybe on the
   table,
Have what he had asked for.

PROTECTION

My friend and I are driving
The flat, black highway
At the base of the mountains
Surrounding Salt Lake
Like a circle of Conestogas
The old settlers pulled into at night
To protect themselves.
Anne says, *Maybe I just dreamed it,*
Meaning she can't trust herself
To hold a memory so clear
It became a fact about her:
The man was not my father.

Days later, I wake from a dream:
My father wants to touch me,
Looks at me the way no father should look
And I say, *No.*
To refuse him in the dream
Is to deny the girl's wish
To be chosen over the mother,
Is to draw a circle
Of women around you
Until that protection itself becomes a kind of prison.

This morning, the man I love
Is outside early,
Nailing a clothesline to the house,
Casting a lean shadow
Like my father's,
Who cast a long line
Into the rivers of my childhood
As I sat on the banks and watched.
And I watch him
As the mother watches the girl
Well up with shame,
Having risen from the bed
Where the dream took place,
As if it had happened.

I HAD A VISION

My friend sees the rows of spindly plants
I've put in along the fence line,
That will grow to be a twelve-foot hedge,
I tell him, the scraggly gaps between them
Making them look lonely, like people standing in line
For a ticket to a movie who try hard not to bump each
      other.

When Tony says, *Karen, this hedge is a vision,*
I do not know what he means. When I look,
I see the hedge eight or ten years from now:
A beautiful forest beyond which there are no neighbors
Working on rusty, broken-down trucks, no street behind
Telegraphed with traffic.

Tony sees *what is,* which makes us different.
He sees *me:* I don't look at the magazines
With starving children peppered with flies,
Those slick covers like advertisements for death
In a foreign country. I'd want to *do* something.

Maybe that's why Tony can see the sadness in everything,
Even my strange friend who, I keep telling Tony,
Is a really nice guy. Tony's wise, because he knows his
      limits

And that the probability I'll still be here when the hedge
Has climbed to its predestined pinnacle
Is almost zero. He carries a platter of chicken in from
    the Weber
Knowing something has died, but we eat it anyway
And didn't we love it, and the talk of good friends?

I side with Tony, but when I look at it this moment
It is thick and lush with birds clapping in the blood-red
    berries,
The way I dreamed it would be.

PICKING PLUMS

August, and the plums come on
Pulling the Japanese branches down, soft as testicles
With the renewing seed inside the sweet sacs.
But this is the end of something:
The trees are turning skeletal
The way women lose their beauty,
The way the sky pinkens at the fringes of the horizon,
As if it can't hold on to the idea of being blue.

It doesn't seem right that I am out here by myself
At the top of this ladder unscrewing the plums.
All my life I've tried to save things
And lost everything instead.
But *let go*, and people go on being themselves
Which is simply the world digging in its heels:
The drunk drinking because that's what he loves
Then getting in the car because he also loves to drive,
The saint praying because he's afraid,
And where would we be without those sobering visions
Of our own possibility?

And so I lift this great sack
Of what is neither borrowed nor stolen, but on my
        property.

I won't give them away this time. *Mine, mine,*
I say to myself because I'm the only one there,
Because I put my ear up to the door of myself, and listen.
And I lift this weight of who I am away from this tree,
Whose loss I bear into the bare house of myself.

THE CALLING

It lit above me
On the top rail of the fence,
An ordinary sparrow
Startling the silence. It fixed a grave eye on me,
Contemplative and curious,
As just that morning I'd watched
A knotted worm untangle itself
From the dirt. *Five inches*
Is as a thousand years of effort,
Said the Buddha of my soul,
While I chipped at the ground with a trowel
And listened to his song.

He saw a pile of green
On the green grass as I plucked weeds
From the green thicket of montbretia.
He saw that I was moving
This green to *that* green
With great care and consideration.

And he cocked his head and shivered
And told me to rise up
And look at what I'd done.

I don't remember whether it was his word
Or mine, but the self
Inside my head was stunned
That my life had made no difference.

AFTER DRIVING BACK
FROM THE CITY

Maybe God is a euphemism
For the parts of the world that are painless
This morning in February
When the spring martins set up housekeeping
In the musky winter rooms
Of the ash trees. I don't want to see anyone
Today—the sorrow of people
Is like a three-legged dog
That hobbled over for a pat
From the customers
In the parking lot of an IGA.
Animals are stoic, a vet once said
Before slipping the sleep into our Labrador's
Ruff. If what he said is true,
I must be stoic,
And the man chopping wood
In the rain must be stoic.

I've learned the various names of birds,
Thinking I needed to know
Something factual, and to define things
More by their differences.
The two martins inhabit the ash

After a season of freezing and rainy mud
Above the drab garden
That pauses under commas of rain.

That girl on The Ave
Who was sitting on the sidewalk
Yesterday asked for a dollar. I pulled out a bill
And saw her, later, unwrapping a cheeseburger
And passing it back and forth, like a smoke
To her lover, his hands in and out of his pockets,
His shoes scuffing at the cement.
I must have thought I owed her something
When she opened her hand.

THE GOOD LIE

Steve Champion lays his head upon his desk
And snores during Spelling. He has
A constant runny nose and purple circles
Under his eyes. His father's socks
Pool below his skinny blue ankles.

Every morning, my mother lays eight slices
Of bread on the counter
As if she's playing solitaire. She pastes
A leaf of lettuce over each slice of bologna
Like the ten over the Jack. She hands me
Two lunches and practices for the hundredth time
How I'm to offer one to Steve,
How *Charity must never demean,*
How *I must lie to spare his dignity.*

At lunch I take the second sandwich
From the paper bag
And hold it out between us
As if I've found his paper on the floor—
Not an act of giving, but returning.
Every day I say the same words, *My mother*
Has made too much for me. Would you like this?
Every day him unwrapping the sandwich

With his unwashed hands and disinterested stare.
My mother worries what will happen to him
As I grow into the role she has assigned me
Like a desk, at which I sit each day
My back ruler-straight, my braids,
My eyes turned dutifully on the teacher,
Thinking, *Fake angel, I want to break you.*

THERE'S A ROSE CALLED
EVERLASTING

All night, you tossed
And spoke from the dream
From which I could not wake you.
Twice, you cried out.

What a relief, this light!
A sack of apples,
A bee weakened by cold weather
Prowling the last of the Gravensteins,
Warm sap filling the porch
With the ripe scent of cider.

My own desire
Makes me sleepy. Three times in the night
I turned toward your animal heat,
Helpless with need.
The bee drunkenly rises
Like the soul of Christ
Whose crime was loneliness.

I've built a little garden
With a rose called *Everlasting*.
I have a white dress.
Lie awake with me tonight.

II.

FAILING FOR YOU

Miss Bush said we would make aprons
First, then difficult pajamas.
We set the pattern on the fabric
And pinned and cut
Until what wasn't meant to come together
Fell away.

We gathered and we tucked
Until the long arms wrapped
Around, a skirt in front.
Still I could not get it right:
The long, loose stitches of a baste,
The tedium of bunching at the hem.

She sent mine home,
A note attached, to ask
Please work until I did it well.
My mother whipped the needle
In and out for half an hour.
The pocket held. The strings got tied.

My mother got an *A*
And made a flowered blouse for me.
And I gave her the apron
She'd assembled with great care,
Her competent hands accepting the gift
As if to mend it.

FAMILY STORY

A cousin I never knew was hit
By a fast car and was dragged and died. I must have been
Six; my mother placed the receiver into its cradle and
    entered
A house of grief where she wailed, for days, as if it had
    happened
To her, not to the mother in the story.

I knew that children don't really die, not forever, but my
    father
Packed his best suit and shoes and his brown leather
Shaving kit into the small suitcase. He flew to
Atlanta for the funeral,
His Baptist family together again
Joining hands beside the baptismal river
Like links in their chain of sorrow.

My mother left no detail untold:
The strewn body patched together
By the local undertaker, the driver
Torn open by grief and guilt, set free.

I stood outside the circle that story made, with no means
To understand or give it meaning, and I watched my
　　　mother,
Without dignity or empathy, forget that there were other
Lesser people, at that moment, lifting the small coffin.

UNDER THE SIGN OF FIRE

Obsessive, I grieve the end
Of each day, each book I read,
Each bowl of morning yogurt rinsed clean.
I hate the word *over*
Whether it's a minute or a season.

A man once called me *melodramatic.*
I don't think so. So what if I broke
Like porcelain over that table,
The flame of the candle between him and me,
Making a wave in a glass dome, his face
Stripped of all its defenses, like a child's
Rising from sleep when I asked him
What he expected of me. Struck
Dumb, he couldn't answer.

I am red-haired; I was born
Under the sign of fire
And I burn with such intensity
No one will touch me.
My life is a torch
That consumes everything I want or love.

At four o'clock, the courthouse
Tower sounds as many bells.
The little evening birds begin
Their sad, sweet repetitions,
Like a girl practicing piano.
The hammer strikes the strings
And the elemental air,
Which also feeds the fire,
Carries the endless noises of the world,
And fuels the flaming sorrow in me.

BELOW ZERO

At night, in the warm pipes
Beneath the house, in the dark tunnels
Under the iron grids of the vents,
A small soft body claws.

It moves from one end of the bedroom
To the other, neither fast nor furious
But trapped. I imagine a mouse,
A rat maybe, burrowed up through some small
Opening expecting to find food or nest
Or a field leading to others of its kind,
But I am not its kind.

By morning, it is gone
The floorboards beneath me empty
And only the clock's audible increments
Of time pushing me forward from stove
To sink to dishes and, at last, my desk
Where, relieved in this bright light
There is nothing I have to kill or to save.

A DIFFERENT LANGUAGE

All I want is a soda
From the Chinese take-out booth
In the mall. The woman
Behind the register doesn't speak English
But points to the Coke sign
Above her, a flashing neon flag
The one word we both know.

The woman holds up six fingers
And I count two quarters
And a dime from my fuchsia leather
Coin pouch, which seems like a scream
Lying there, under the dignified gaze
Of the waitress,
Her precise hands pushing the buttons
And the register bell ringing
Like a signal from the kitchen
That the shrimp is ready.

She slides a soda across the counter
And smiles until, somehow, I feel we're friends
As I sit outside the mall
On a bench and sip my Coke
Through a red and white striped straw

Like a kid sucking a candy cane.
Pigeons peck around my feet
For bread, but I don't have any.
We all are willing to make trades:
People bow to each other,
And my dog, at home,
Knows to lift one paw for a biscuit.

HEAVENLY COMPLETION

Even though I know it's rude
To do this, to stare so unabashedly
At someone I barely know
And, in fact, have never met
I cannot take my eyes off him,
The old man bending over sausage
And a biscuit, the age-tremor,
The muscle-thing, he's ventured forth
Into the world in spite of.

And he almost falls asleep,
A little drop of spittle falling
Deftly, almost tenderly, down his chin
Before he jerks himself awake
And blinks at what is spread
So lavishly before him, the meal
Like the Christ-meal,
Like the last one you'll ever get,
So that if you fall asleep, so what?
It's all you have to do on this ordinary morning
And it's like mowing the lawn.

If it isn't perfection you're into
Who cares that you have to rest a little
In between—whether the long aisles of grass
Or the slow bites, the thick bites,
It's just the doing of it:
The push and breathe and rest and rest,
The almost there before it's over,
The last bite, the heavenly completion
That makes you want to do it again.

FAMILY OF HARD WORKERS

I would like to forget
That I come from a family of hard workers:
Grandfather of axe handles carved
For the Georgia railroad, Grandmother
Of thirteen children flinging feed for the chickens
From a fifty-pound bag, forgive me,
I forget you. And if my father glorifies
What is, in actuality, a certain lack of choices
On the part of his relatives
Who rose at the cock's crow
And made a day so similar to the one before it
That if someone asked what they'd done that day,
They would stand with their hands in their pockets
Then give you their one answer:
I whittled an axe handle. I fed the chickens.
Then, forgive me for not doing that, too.

Once, I kept a carved statue of a horse
On my window sill,
The right front leg crooked, like a little finger
Which made the horse seem always in motion.
It's all I remember about the horse,
The arched leg ready to step
Into the green pastures of my imagination

And thrum with its hooves,
Churning up grass, unhaltered, unsaddled,
Its huge head rivening the wind.
Better if my father had said:
You come from a family
Where beauty matters.
Look at the horse, now,
Running for joy.

EQUINOX

The first day of spring
Knocks at the door
With official green papers—
Pussywillows' dewclaws turn velvet;
Skunk cabbage pulls yellow scarves
From its sleeves in the marsh.

My life seems like retirement
As the dog springs ahead of me.
But each house on the block
Has its phantoms of tragedy:
The epileptic son who will turn forty
This year, the widow burning twigs
In the pail beside the road.

When I was a child, I used to want
To be *that flower or that bird*—
Either rooted or free
But graceful as I bent to earth
Like the arms of a dancer.

A steel band playing
On the corner of Fifth and Union
Two summers ago still taps its toe inside my blood,

And I remember a father
Leading his daughter into a cha-cha
And how the crowd stepped back
To make a dance floor
On the cobbled street
And how, afterward, the child cried
Having eaten her crust of joy.

BARGAIN

Her hands flash with diamonds
On the buttons of the till, though her faded uniform,

Her blue-veined legs, her bartender's husky voice
As she calls each customer *Hon*, do not confirm

The wealth that makes her hands seem laden.
I see these women everywhere:

The night clerk at the all-night food mart,
The hairdresser whose nails, like dark moons

Are stained with dye, and now this waitress
Who shoves a paper cup beneath the nipple

Of the espresso machine, bejeweled and gemmed
Enough to be a queen.

Maybe her husband works the graveyard shift
At the local airplane factory, his face behind

The welder's mask, for a paycheck and a pension.
Their small yard would be absent of flowers

The curtains drawn as night passes into day
Then back to night again. And maybe the days

Are a compulsion to avoid the terror
Of a life where there is never enough

And the terrible excesses gnaw.
And now she extends the cup to me. These rings

Cannot conceal the face, lined and tired,
Where beauty might once have lived, where a life turned

And some emptiness set in, as the soul
Began to bargain for its losses.

NEIGHBORS

At midnight, yesterday's argument
Is waxing into tomorrow's
And their voices, muffled, as if under water,
Sharpen to pierce the thin walls
Of their house to enter the open bedroom
Window, where I leave the dream
To answer the alarm.

Like a fire, they are raging and it
Is sexual: *Why don't we ever do it, anymore?*
And the woman overweight and pasty and
Pregnant with a third child gives back
As good as she gets, screaming
Bastard. Screaming, *You're fucking nuts.*

And now the baby is awake
And the older daughter is trying to calm them all,
The competent hand of reason sorting
The pile of dirty laundry they've made of their lives.
Too old for her own good, her homework
Lies open and undone
On the sticky kitchen table where they will sit,
Hours from now, housed in their separate angers
And complaints, hurt, abandoned to each other
Over chipped bowls of cold cereal.

How bland the world must seem to them
With its various and complimentary orders:
Each street lined by rows of kept houses,
The same species of cherry tree fogged
With blossoms stitching the green aisles of the parking
        strips,
And the grind of the garbage truck
Opening its jaws in the Tuesday pre-dawn.

The girl leaves the house,
Mussed and rumpled, slightly
Apprehensive as the bus idles at the corner
With its tribe of teasers, pranksters and yellers,
And the over-aged mean boy at the back.
She enters last, as if the minutes between that door
And this door were the grace of hesitation.

MOTHER OF A SON

She doesn't want to talk
About it, the son in the cemetery,
The third, the one who refused to outlast her.
She knows where his bed is—
Under the green blanket. She changes
The flowers beside it, like a bandage.
Bad enough that it happened,
She says. To tell more would make it
Happen again, would put the tree
In the elbow crook of the dark road.

It has emptied her, this grief, like Mary
Who knew when he went into the desert
That thirst would blister him more.
That stone for a pillow
Would bruise him more.
How she must have hated
That angel, who lay atop her
In the dark. The child, always looking upward,

Loved the clouds' changing shapes
And thought he saw his father there.
How eagerly he climbed the cross
Like a train that would bear him
To what, all his life, he'd longed for:
Mercy from the voices, from feeling torn.

Mary must have been so bent
As his soul undressed, his body slumped like a shirt
On the nails. Not a single bird circled.
She must have known it would end like this.
She must have dizzied, as she did
That night in the straw, God's horrible angel coming.

WAITING OUTSIDE

It is cool here
In the shade of the elms
Parked outside the doctor's office
With the windows rolled down
And a breeze passing through
On its way to who knows where?
With the ease of an old friend talking
On a back porch
The breeze, intent on itself
Says nothing but its own name.
And the couple having breakfast
Begins to speak in low, gravelly tones
On the deck behind the elms,
Behind the leaf-shine and wing-flicker.

Her voice carries a hurt in it and his
Leans on the two back legs of its chair
And studies her with stoniness.
Her words circle on their heels
And walk back into the house,
Having done with the bowl of oranges,
The cold triangles of toast, the pretty pot
Of coffee.

I'm not part of this argument.
If I saw this couple on the street
I would not know who they were.
Maybe she'd be the one woman
In the crowded café with long vermilion nails
And a face set tight around a hard mouth.
And maybe he'd be slipping a quarter
Into a newspaper box
And some efficiency of gesture,
A crisp fold of the paper
Like the clipped edge to what he had said
Would make me think it's him, and maybe not.
And me, I just lie back into the hammock
Of my thoughts of how they must be dressing
To go out, now, into something ordinary,
Wanting to look like they belong
To the world.

BROKEN BONE

Because I could not walk
Without the crutches,
The bone in my hip broken
And needing the least weight
To repair, my husband lowered me into the tub,
Then quietly left—whether in shame or in pity
I do not know. And after I had bathed,
My body no longer mine,
I called, and he came from some brooding room
Of the house, and, again, looking away
Held out the thick towel
As I rose from the water
On one strong leg.

We barely spoke,
The damp kindling refusing to catch.
And when my husband
Slept beside me, some sixth sense
Kept him still, while the bone
Sent out its Morse code of healing
And the blood engineered its bridge.
All winter, the bone
Branched toward its other half
And the sap sang a green song in the trees.

AFTER THE REJECTION

The world is still what it is: a shaped and colored map
Telling us where we are. You didn't get
To see the tree, the oldest living tree
Here, leaning a little toward the north,
Its branches tracing roads against an indigo sky
And at the end of each
There are no more choices to be made.
Dead center, an apple the size of a cherry
Over-wintered. It didn't grow
And it didn't fall, always a bud—
What good is a bud?—always the unblinking eye
At the heart of any city.
But the bud is what you wanted,
The closed fist of it, systolic,
Refusing to *become*. I don't mind.
I am still what I am. I open and open,
Diastolic, and afterward the ascension,
Meaning, I stopped the fall.

IRON LUNG

Keith has polio, and his parents
Wheel him through the white doors
Of the Baptist church on Cherry Hill.
They sell their house
To take him to Oral Roberts
But he comes back, looking ashen and sad.
We lift his thin hands;
We race the wheelchair down the holy halls.

A glass booth in the alcove
Of the Lincoln Theater,
A blue-eyed, life-sized doll
Sleeping inside, like a Russian princess.
Polio will make a doll of you,
Someone whispers to their daughter.

Old Yeller is showing at the Lincoln.
When the dog gets shot,
I want to go home. Tube lights
Illuminate the fake child
As we walk outside. It looks warm
In there. She seems religious.

READING THE UGLY DUCKLING

Another world opened, then
  With something called *Hope* in it.

I was ten
  And didn't know what makes

The heart in a young girl rise
  Is not *what is*, but *what might be.*

All freckles and red braids,
  Thin as a blade

And quick, I would race the boys
  Across the open, calling fields

And play dolls with the girls,
  As if I could choose one gender

Or the other at that androgynous age
  Of sexual innocence.

I watched my mother in silk stockings
  Dazzle my father, a diamond

Brooch at her throat and the sweep of Evening
   In Paris daubed

At each pulse point
   Before she slipped into the jacket

He held out to her, then stepped through the door.

Page by illustrated page, in the lamplight
   Of the living room

I saw nature work her magic
   On the squat scrawny duckling

Who returned one day to the pond
   In her white cloak of feathers,

Her slender swan's neck poised
   Into a perfect semblance of a question mark—

Oh!—she glided silently across the lake
   Beyond the pages, and I closed the book

And waited for the transformation.

WHEN HE PRUNES THE ROSES

From the upstairs window
I watch him unload the long-handled shovel
And the rusty bucket from the old truck's bed,
Listen to him unlock the white gate
And begin to clip;
His scissors are like a latch
Opening and closing under me.

I can tell, when he moves,
Just where he is
In what part of the garden:
Louder, now in the red Jessica,
Fainter in the Old Blush from China.
What would bring a man
Who was once a logger
To tend old roses?
He bends over the bed
Taking in the intimacy of scent
The white Albas release.
Clearly, he is lingering,
Taking what he can from the canes
Until the shade shifts
And he flickers in and out of light
Hauling away the cut stalks.

You should see him, how he touches
The petals, like panties in his hands—
Pink and white and red
As he loosens them,
Dropping them into this blue bandana,
Then folding it over.

IN THE LAP OF A STRANGER

A young man is bending
Over an old man
Lying on a street corner
At the busiest intersection
Of the city.
Homeless or drunk, I can't tell which,
But there are hundreds of us passing
And only one man stops,
Cradles that dirty head
Between his knees.

It's the soles of the shoes
Turned up that make me want
To turn away—so small!
The feet pointing like arrows
Straight up and motionless,
And the crosswalk box's little man
Walking in his mechanical way,
As if on a treadmill,
And the man not walking,
Not getting up.

When the light changes,
We all drive through,
Going forward into appointments,
Shopping and errands like a future,
Choosing the crispest head of lettuce
At the grocer's, which will taste
Particularly sharp tonight.
Glad for awhile it wasn't us
Saying our goodbyes
To our one and only life, in public,
In second-hand clothes,
Easing through the ethers
Into the afterlife
From the lap of a stranger
We've probably made late.

SOUNDS THAT COME TO HER PORCH IN EVENING

There, a bench,
And she is sitting on it
Thinking how the length
Of it suggests waiting,
Like waiting for a train.

Behind a steadiness of hills,
Old moon only half-risen.

From the house
Two miles above her,
A harmonica begins
Bluesing out a song—
Lips pressing up the mouthpiece,
Metal cupped in both palms.

There comes a little religion
Then, a pasture-quiet inside her.
Tall field grasses
Bend under music
And one note is held so long,
It whistles through her,
Hawk ruffling the twilight pines.

SUMMER FLOOD

The gods don't like to be ignored.
Too many days of shining weather
And tonight's obsidian split open,
A knife of light, and rain
Streaming the panes of the house.

Forty days and forty nights
Before the dove flapped upward.
I wait for a word
Between pulses, the backyard lit by lightening
Then the neighbor's house, and beyond,
The pastures
With the big-boned cattle,
Their faces like spilled milk.

To see all this, then nothing,
And to stand and from the window
Breathless, see it all again,
To want and want
A world with shapes, republic of definition.
I need a gull or two
To blow in, off the choppy water.
I need someone

Stomping on the porch,
Someone coming home
Seeing the house lit up
Off the Bay Loop road.

DISCOVERY BAY, 1960

We dress in the dark,
Drive in the dark
To be early on the beach
Where the most clams burrow.
My father has a shovel and a bucket
And balances one in each hand
As my mother hurries after him
Carrying a basket of hard eggs
And oranges. A shell, a rind
I love to peel away
Then the crumbly, yellow yolk
Inside the white, like happiness.
Eat, my mother says,
It's hours before lunch.

Those sharp words that pass
Between them, too often lately,
Those blues will be left unsung.
There is nothing to cut away
In a dawn this lovely
As the dark doesn't lift, exactly,
But gives water back, gives eyesight.

My brother finds a trick
Like a stick on the beach—
His forefinger dimples the sand
And we double every clam hole
With a facsimile of it.
There is no difference anyone can see,
And my parents try five times
Before even one clam
Spits its pitiful defense,
A salty arc of fear.

We don't say a word.
The pail barely fills
With a hoof, a strike, a count
Against the metal sides.
There's a sound for emptiness.
There is no punishment
We don't think of.
The consequence? The lie
My father goes down two feet for,
The shovels full of nothing
He lifts as he lifts.

THE HAIRCUT

Pine Street, 1960. My mother's sheets
Filling with wind on the clothesline
Father's built, catching and releasing
The morning air, like huge, white gulls.
Pansies, Mother's favorite flower,
Nod beneath the eaves
Out of the wilting sun.

My hair is past my waist
And Mother carries a chair
From the kitchen to the grass—chrome
With yellow vinyl. I'm fidgeting
But she promises an hour at the playground
So I sit in my churchly posture, hands folded
Beneath the towel, ankles crossed.
I can't hold this still.
I can't be this good.

She brushes back my hair, hard
Until I yelp at the thick knot the teeth
Of the comb can't unlatch;
The scissors whisper near my ear
And a heavy swatch of red
Collapses on the grass. The strands refract—
Gold and orange and brown.

I can't see her hands, my head is bowed,
And there's a dull scuff on the toe
Of my brown oxford, a flat nickel in the shine.
My neck prickles where the long hair falls
Rope by rope away. I can't see me now
But I know I've lost something,
Some ballast that kept me anchored
To earth. I will float away, like a balloon
A child's hand forgets in the carnival crowd.
I will float away. I can't see me, now.

THE RENTED VIOLIN

Not the music of Mozart
Rising neat as a made bed

From the resined bow,
But rudimentary scales

Lurching from the strings
As my unpracticed hands

Bore the indentations of steel.
Between my chin and shoulder

A rented violin,
A sick bird singing in the cage,

Sawed and stuttered.
How taut the body

Becomes with its impediments
Until the stiff wrist

Learns its lesson: resistance
Is a stone. And in that sparse room

Sitting on the bed, the door staunched
Against my parents' argument

Thinking, *Make it beautiful*
And it will save you,

Afternoon stammered into evening,
And I loosed myself

Into the swaying silk of the bow.

DECAY

Painted black to attract heat,
Like an oven in which eggshells,
Fruit rinds and garlic's dried fingernails
Have baked and simmered all winter,
It seems simple to drop the pail
Of peelings in, turn it with a rake
And forget that it is there.

When I was a child reading
The Diary of Anne Frank, I envied
That family stored behind a wall
Of an attic, safely away from the world.
Later, learning about the camps, the teacher
Explained to us ash and human bones
Rose from those factories,
Though no one had chosen it.
The few survivors, orphaned and widowed
Searched everywhere, asking, *Have you seen my brother?*
Do you know my sister?

When there is no one left to cling to,
No one to fall on sobbing in mutual recognition
When it's over, maybe we cling to the world
That hurt us, seeing the face of someone
We loved in the face of someone we don't know,
Hallucinating a figure, there
Beyond the smoke of the empty burning yard.

NOTES & ACKNOWLEDGMENTS

Thanks to the editors of the following journals, where these poems first appeared:

Harvard Review: "The Calling"
Blue Unicorn: "Hollyhocks"
Passages North: "Falling," "Love Must Be Actual"
Bellowing Ark: "Sounds that Come to Her Porch in
        Evening"
Shades: "Under the Sign of Fire," "Family of Hard
        Workers," "When He Prunes the Roses,"
        "A Different Language," "French Rose"

With special thanks to Anne Caston for her friendship and careful reading of these poems and to George Allison for his constancy.

With gratitude to all my teachers: Debra Allberry, Brooks Haxton, Tony Hoagland, Heather McHugh, and to the community of writers at Warren Wilson College, particularly Ellen Voigt for her quiet strength and continuous support.

Finally, thanks to all my friends, writers and otherwise, who keep me on course: Christine Hale, Bethany Reid,

Marian Szczepanski, Hansi Hals and Tom Butler, Jean and Alan Bentsen, Jennifer Nixon, and my sister, LaDell Curtin.

I thank the Rona Jaffee Foundation for giving me the time to write these poems. Bob Martin, Director of the Department of Community Development, arranged a leave of absence so that I could make use of the Jaffe Award. My thanks to him, as well.